Making Money Online Guide for Beginners

Learn How to Easily Make $5000/Month Passive Income Online Money by Making Money from Home

Victoria Heart

© **Copyright 2014 by Joy Publishing & Marketing Corporation - All rights reserved.**

This document is geared towards providing helpful and reliable information in regards to the topic and issue covered. The publication is sold with the idea that the publisher is not required to render accounting, officially permitted, or otherwise, qualified services. If advice is necessary, legal or professional, a practiced individual in the profession should be ordered.

- From a Declaration of Principles which was accepted and approved equally by a Committee of the American Bar Association and a Committee of Publishers and Associations.

In no way is it legal to reproduce, duplicate, or transmit any part of this document in either electronic means or in printed format. Recording of this publication is strictly prohibited and any storage of this document is not allowed unless with written permission from the publisher. All rights reserved.

The information provided herein is stated to be truthful and consistent, in that any liability, in terms of inattention or otherwise, by any usage or abuse of any policies, processes, or directions contained within is the solitary and utter responsibility of the recipient reader. Under no circumstances will any legal responsibility or blame be held against the publisher for any reparation, damages, or monetary loss due to the information herein, either directly or indirectly.

Respective authors own all copyrights not held by the publisher.

The information herein is offered for informational purposes solely, and is universal as so. The presentation of the information is without contract or any type of guarantee assurance.

The trademarks that are used are without any consent, and the publication of the trademark is without permission or backing by the trademark owner. All trademarks and brands within this book are for clarifying purposes only and are the owned by the owners themselves, not affiliated with this document.

Table of Contents

Introduction	1
8 Benefits of Making Money from Home	3
10 Methods of Earning $5000/Month of Income at Home	7
Conclusion	21
One Last Thing	23

Introduction

I want to thank you and congratulate you for purchasing the book, ***Making Money Online Guide for Beginners:*** *Learn How to Easily Make $5000/Month Passive Income Online Money by Making Money from Home.*

This book contains proven steps and strategies on how to earn $5000 worth of passive income from within the comfort of your home.

Because this book is aimed for beginners, I focused on ten of the most in-demand home-based money-making opportunities today – from online classes to B&Bs (or Bed & Breakfast services) to gourmet & organic foods to call centers. Anything and everything you need to know about getting into this industry is stated in **Making Money Online Guide for Beginners**.

Thanks again for purchasing this book, I hope you enjoy it! Please take some time to stop by and LIKE our Facebook page:

https://www.facebook.com/joypublishing

With gratitude,

Victoria Heart

8 Benefits of Making Money from Home

Each and every one of us desires to become successful in life by working in a more comfortable atmosphere. In this day and age, many people prefer to work on their own while wearing pajamas – thanks to home-based and online businesses! Earning $5000 via the internet is one of the most popular yet easiest ways of generating significant income. However, it still requires the same amount of consistency, patience, and hard-work as that of office-based duties.

Benefits of Making Money from Home

1. **Interviews and prior experience are not necessary**

    This is the very first thing you'll get a sigh of relief from. In home-based businesses, no one will ask you those tricky questions (i.e. relating your desired job to the degree you finished, why did you choose this job despite a lack of experience in this and that, etc.) Working from the comfort of home gives you a chance to choose your own job. The only thing you need here is a creative mindset. That simply means having the passion for doing stuff suitable to your interests.

2. **It allows you to take control of your expenses**

    Budget plays a crucial role in any kind of job. It's a big deal if we're keeping a tight budget schedule. You need to take control of your daily expenses by being a wise spender.

    In home-based jobs, you don't need to settle travel expenses. In other words, you don't need passes for transportation or to drive your car. Additionally, incidental expenses are lowered when you consider working at home.

3. **It guarantees flexible timing**

   Punctuality is very important while at work. Unfortunately, several companies go beyond the rule of letting their employees work on time. When you're late by just a minute, you'll immediately get a reprimand from your boss.

   But working at home promises none of that. You can work anytime based on your availability. You can work 24/7 or two times a week. In making money at home, **you are your own boss.**

4. **There is no dress code**

   Most of the time, you need to be in proper work attire, typically corporate wear, during office hours. In home-based jobs however, you don't need that. You can even work while you're in your pajamas. Just make sure you don't use Skype or any video conferencing programs when conversing with your suppliers and customers or else they won't think you're serious enough to deal with.

5. **It allows you to connect yourself more with the world**

   If you're working in an office, you see the same people and do the same job which brings about boredom most of the time. But if you're working from home, you're learning and doing stuff which can be exciting in many ways.

Social media has become an effortless option for making money from home. Many home-based individuals prefer to connect with people via Facebook, Twitter or Tumblr in earning money.

6. There is less pressure in deciding on your salary

In home-based jobs, you can earn as much as you want. Work for two or 48 hours, and the money is all yours 100%. There is no tax deduction required unlike in offices (wherein if you work beyond the given office hours, you'll typically only get 70% of your salary because the 30% will go to taxes).

7. It warrants long-term income

Working from home guarantees you long-term income as long as you put in a lot of consistency and hard work. You can earn more than $5000 in one month if you're not just focusing on a particular field (which is, of course, your choice).

8. There is less stress

Stress is the most common health problem occurring among office-based employees. Almost 80% of people going to offices suffer from stress because of heavy demands from their bosses.

When you work at home, stress is not a big deal. As the stress levels in your body go down, you become more at ease and happy with what you're doing.

10 Methods of Earning $5000 Worth of Income At Home

There are hundreds of legitimate ways of making money from home. Some of them involve putting up your own business while others involve working with certain individuals.

In this chapter, we'll discuss the most in-demand methods of earning $5000/month worth of income at home today.

a) Medical Transcription

If you have excellent computer skills and knowledge in the field of medicine, this job is for you. Most doctors are in need of people who can transcribe their notes for patients. However, some of them are not paying the exact $5000 to transcriptionists. Doctors usually farm out their work so they prefer transcriptionists who have finished a degree in medicine.

Requirements:

Training – To become a full-time medical transcriptionist, you need to undergo further training. As stated above, most doctors prefer degree holders in medicine so if you make the cut, it wouldn't be hard for you to transcribe notes. You need to be proficient in medical terminologies, though.

Note: For non-medical degree holders, you can take short courses for just $2500.

Equipment – When you get a job from a highly-reputable company, they will provide you the equipment necessary except for high-speed internet connection. In line with this, beware of medical transcription services that require you to provide your own equipment because that is indicative of a scam.

Socialize – Before you start working, you need to establish contacts who are veterans in the job. They can serve as your mentors – keeping you updated with the dos and don'ts of the job. In landing a medical transcription gig at home, you can look for contacts via the *Association for Healthcare Documentation Integrity* website.

b) Consultants

Home-based consultants use the World Wide Web in offering their services for a minimal fee. For example, you can be a consultant for a non-profit organization. You can help them develop their fundraising plans and oversee their outcome. You can also help out a newly-established company gain media attention by writing press releases and distributing them to networks.

Individuals hire home-based consultants, too. They rely on such consultants for financial advice while others pay them to do the job of setting up or maintaining their household.

Requirements:

Work space – When working as a consultant from home, there are possibilities that clients will visit you personally. That being said, you need a wide and neat home office. Set up your work space in a secluded area that is very welcoming to guests (If you want to, you can use your garage.) Take note that a clean and spacious home office adds to your credibility.

Marketing skills – When working as a consultant, you don't need to market your services; you need to market yourself. You'll have to "brand" yourself in a way that people will trust you. For example, if you're branding yourself as a marketing consultant, try asking yourself why a person should trust you with his life savings then figure out some ways to convey it to other potential customers (i.e. sales letter, portfolio, brochures etc.).

Prior experience – Whatever area you want to focus on as a consultant, you must have a knack for advising clients very effectively. If you're consulting for organizations that are close to your field, make sure you are an active member.

c) Book Sales

You can earn $5000 from selling old paperbacks you have at home. Not everyone can afford a new book to read, and home-based individuals are selling their books via AbeBooks, eBay, Goodreads or Amazon. They use online scanners in determining how long it takes for a particular book to sell and how much it will sell for.

Requirements:

Storage – No matter how big or small your business is, you need storage for the books. Having storage keeps them in good condition thus making it easier for you to find them when someone will buy.

Finances – To earn $5000 from books, you must have a knack for quick decision-making and mathematics. You need to be wary of how much you pay for the books and tracking your expenses after a day of selling them. When you choose to sell online, the site will take a commission from your regular sales. eBay charges a listing fee for every book that is sold.

Ratings – When someone purchases a book from you, a rating transaction should be granted. When we talk about ratings in home-based selling, this has something to do with telling other potential customers whether the book was mailed on time or kept under a condition you described.

Shipping – This applies to online book sellers. You'll only have a few days to ship the book after it was sold. In some cases, it can even be less than a day if you considered "Overnight Shipping."

Note: If you want a cheaper option of sending books, try "Media Mail".

d) Sewing Services

If you're good at sewing, then this home-based job is for you. This is one of the most unique jobs we have today. Here, you can do a variety of designs and alterations out of custom-made clothes, wedding dresses, and other special attires.

The job also lets you design upholstery cushions, draperies, customized beddings, bags and totes. You can take your services to the next level by sewing special canvas cushions necessary for chairs, tables and even small boats!

Requirements:

Zoning – Because this job involves a lot of people negotiating in and out of your home, you need to check with your local authorities first. This is to determine whether you need to be zoned in the business or not.

Equipment – One of the most important pieces of equipment you need in this job is a sewing machine. The high quality ones range in price from $3000 to $7000. Other pieces of equipment needed may vary, depending on what you want to focus on. For example, if you want to focus on making custom draperies, you need a drapery steamer and serger.

Promotion – To let people know about your sewing services, one of the best ways is to promote it. You can start with the basics of letting your family and friends know about your business first, then it would be up to them if they'll promote it to others. Make sure your friends are aware of what you're offering. You can also promote your services via Facebook (which may be the easiest method for targeting many customers today).

Skills – This job requires you to possess excellent skills in sewing any kind of clothes for people. For beginners, you need to improve your sewing skills before attempting to make money from this business. The more skilled you are, the faster you can produce quality work, thus giving you enough time to accept and then deliver more orders from customers.

e) Call Centers

In this day and age, you can become a call center agent at your own home. All you need is a PC with a high-speed internet connection, a good telephone voice, and the capability to organize information quickly. Call centers (also referred to as *Business Process Outsourcing*) cater to businesses that don't have representatives who can respond to phone calls every day. In this industry, the calls are routed to a company before sending them out to individuals working at their homes. Call center agents are provided with computers, software programs, and telecommunication devices to answer queries from customers.

In the United States, the minimum amount for every call received is $10/hour. Some call center companies offer health and 401k plans for their home-based employees.

Requirements:

Grace under pressure – Let's face it. Being in a call center (either at home or in the office) is a stressful job. You'll get tons of calls from customers (some of whom can be a pain in the neck) so you must have the ability to handle them smoothly.

Diligence – In this business, the line between honesty and fooling people is sometimes blurred. Furthermore, you need to do some homework before getting a position. To know more about how this thing works, contact the *Better Business Bureau* in your community.

Ambition – The opportunities you'll get from being a home-based call center agent are countless. One of these is that you can be your own team leader or account manager. All you need is to become goal-oriented and maintain a positive attitude.

f) Arts & Crafts

If you want to earn $5000 from your creative masterpieces, then this business is for you. The demand for homemade arts and crafts is apparent these days so more people are now considering this as a home-based opportunity.

ETSY is one of the fastest-growing business sites that give artists a chance to sell their items for an affordable price. The site covers over 100 categories – from edibles to clothes to paintings.

Requirements:

Commitment – Most people running home-based art & craft services claim that they do more than what they create. They distribute business cards in various places, they write about it on their blogs, and spend most of their free time finding innovative ways of promoting it. To become successful in this field, you have to treat it like a full-time job.

Research – In any type of business, you need to know what others are selling before deciding on what you want to offer. A lot of people sell handmade products – true! But those who exert enough effort in ensuring their items are unique are the ones who truly stand out. The secret is to **research every day.**

Selections – One of the keys to become successful in this field is having proper selection. Have at least 300 items for sale – each beautifully crafted by you. Having all those items crafted by you is a larger-than-life commitment. Nonetheless, the more options you give to your potentials, the bigger chances of generating massive sales.

Photos – Because your customers won't be able to touch or hold your items immediately, it's important that you should show them photos first. These should be very pleasing in the eye. You can hire a professional photographer or someone who simply loves taking pictures.

g) Gourmet & Organic Foods

Online farmer's markets are becoming in-demand among people who want to eat organic and gourmet foods. Because not all groceries and supermarkets sell such food items, there are people selling rare foods (i.e. tomato pesto, blue goat cheese, balsamic vinegar etc.) via the internet. This is one home-based opportunity that surely a lot of stay-at-home moms might want to consider in the future.

Requirements:

Tools – You need a cash box (for income organization), scale (for food measurement), and other tools you can use for transporting your products.

Display – Just like other retail operations, the method of displaying wares also matters in the home-based industry. Make sure the foods you're selling are placed underneath a tight cover for protection. Display your prices clearly. You can personalize your offers with signs so that it won't confuse your customers.

Rules – All farmers' markets have rules every customer should follow. In putting up an online home-based market, you need to file an application from a market manager in your area before selling.

License – As long as you're selling fresh products only, you don't need to obtain a license. But if you're going to sell gourmet products too, you need to obtain one from health authorities. In the US, the provisions of getting a license for an online food market vary by state.

h) Bed & Breakfast Services

Earning $5000 by hosting people in your house? That's very possible! Many overnight travelers are looking for a typical house to stay in instead of paying $200-$400 for hotel services. If your house is more attractive than those fancy hotel rooms, then this business is absolutely for you!

The best part of having bed & breakfast services is that customers are more likely to pay higher amounts for the experience. The worst part, though, is that competition in this niche is stiff.

Requirements:

Food – In this business, food matters a lot! Some B&Bs serve their guests fresh juice, brewed coffee, and muffins for breakfast. In fact, a lot of successful B&B hosts claim that serving sumptuous breakfasts and dinners creates a lasting impression among guests. However, you can serve any kind of food if you're not catering to certain types of guests.

Comfort – The most important thing you need to become a successful B&B host is by making sure your guests are as comfortable as possible. As stated above, take note that they're paying a higher amount for the experience.

Location – The most successful B&B services are those that are very convenient to tourist attractions and airports, simply because there are two types of guests frequenting B&Bs: families or friends looking for a unique overnight experience and business travelers looking for more relaxation. But this is not to say your home should be located beside an airport or a famous historical spot.

For as long as it provides the right atmosphere for these guests, that's already a plus!

Services – One of the key aspects of becoming successful in this business is by keeping up your standards of servicing. Always remember that you're not just selling a room but an experience. As a B&B host, it is your job to make your guests feel like they're in the comfort of their home.

i) Online Classes

Another awesome way to earn $5000 (or more) at home is by putting up an online classroom. People are willing to pay huge amounts of money to learn various field of knowledge – from home decorating to gardening to baking. The most in-demand courses available today are dog training, dancing, child birthing, playing musical instruments, and foreign languages.

Requirements

Being successful at conducting your own classes at home requires a lot of serious planning and paying attention to every detail. The rest are stated below.

Schedule – Decide first on how often you'll be conducting classes. If you'll be teaching foreign languages for example, you need to have structured classes that often meet at the same day weekly. But if you'll be conducting cooking lessons, that isn't necessary. Remember that in this job you are making a commitment that lasts in weeks or months and you don't want to end up cancelling your classes. Pick a schedule that you can maintain.

Ideas – Because people want to know what they're going to get from the money they paid, it will be up to you how you will explain to them. Be concise and encouraging in using terms and sharing ideas to your students. Understand what you're teaching.

Price – When setting a price for your classes, begin by figuring out other choices your students or clients have in mind. If you are conducting cooking lessons, try to contact in-home teachers. If necessary, compare your experiences to what they're offering. Set a price according to standards given by your community.

Deals – In addition to setting a price, offer deals in enticing people to enroll in your class. Here's an example: If you're going to conduct classes on soap-making, offer them individually. Someone might want to learn how to use fresh flowers on making soap while others prefer to use herbs. When you decide on pricing your classes, always take into consideration the student's side in learning a lot using his money.

Advertisements – key to become successful in this business lies beneath your ability in getting the word out regarding your classes. Don't just depend on your family or friends in promoting your classes. Post fliers and distribute brochures in schools, churches, bookstores and supermarkets. You can also advertise your business in your blog or Facebook page.

j) Freelance Writing

This is the #1 home-based moneymaking opportunity a lot of people are looking into.

Today's freelance writing services cover a wide range of markets. That means you can write for print, web content, or both. You can put up your own site and hire writers or apply at any writing site available.

Requirements:

Tools – Being a freelance writer doesn't require overworking, but there are certain tools you should have. The most important one is a computer, followed by internet connection and knowledge in using word processors. In this job, most of your clients require you to submit articles as a Word document so always make sure that any word processing software you're using is compatible with MS Word.

Writing samples – You need to provide writing samples before marketing yourself. Figure out which market/s you want to approach first, and then create writing samples geared towards your intended market/s. This is the most important thing you need in order to land a freelance writing gig.

Job boards – *oDesk, Freelancer, eLance* and *Guru* are four among the hundreds of freelance writing sites you can be part of. oDesk alone is more than just a writing community; it also allows home-based individuals to post projects for other freelancers to bid them. Check each site and figure out its pros and cons. The common denominator of these four is that signing up for membership is FREE.

Commitment & Persistence – To become successful in your freelance writing gig, you need to have a great amount of persistence. Remember that this type of business is subjective in many ways. While one may appreciate your writing, the other may not. Therefore, always do your best in writing quality articles.

Hold on to your commitment and persistence – and you'll earn lots of money.

So there you have it! – 10 of the most legitimate ways of earning $5000/month of passive income at home. It's an awesome feeling when you make money from something you're into without leaving your house. Trust the experts!

Conclusion

Thank you again for purchasing this book!

I hope this book was able to help you learn the basics of making money from home through the ten provided methods of earning $5000 worth of passive income.

The next step is to choose which among those methods you want to consider in the future. Make sure that your choice suits your interest/s because that is the best secret to becoming successful in making money at home.

In addition, please remember to check out our Facebook page in order to find other resources and upcoming promotions:

https://www.facebook.com/joypublishing

With sincere thanks,

Victoria Heart

One Last Thing...

Source: Wikipedia

If you believe that this book is worth sharing, would you please take the time to let others know how it affected your life? If it turns out to make a difference in the lives of others, they will be forever grateful to you, as will I.